I0787725

CORAZON CALAMIDAD

Abhijit Naskar is the 21st century Neuroscientist and Poet who has been serving at the forefront of humankind's struggle against inhumanity. As an untiring advocate of mental health and global harmony, he became a beloved best-selling author across the world with his very first book "The Art of Neuroscience in Everything". With his revolutionary contributions in Cognitive and Behavioral Neuroscience Naskar has helped the world tackle the horrors of systemic racism, biases, hate, extremism, discrimination and stereotypes more effectively, because of which he is lovingly hailed by humankind as 'the humanitarian scientist'.

Corazon Calamidad

Obedient to None, Oppressive to None

ABHIJIT NASKAR

Corazon Calamidad: Obedient to None, Oppressive to None

Copyright © 2022 Abhijit Naskar

This is a work of non-fiction

All rights reserved. No part of this publication may be reproduced, distributed, or transmitted in any form or by any means, including photocopying, recording, or other electronic or mechanical methods, without the prior written permission of the author, except in the case of brief quotations embodied in critical reviews and certain other noncommercial uses permitted by copyright law.

An Amazon Publishing Company, 1st Edition, 2022

Printed in the United States of America

ISBN: 9798359309691

Also by Abhijit Naskar

The Art of Neuroscience in Everything
Your Own Neuron: A Tour of Your Psychic Brain
The God Parasite: Revelation of Neuroscience
The Spirituality Engine
Love Sutra: The Neuroscientific Manual of Love
Homo: A Brief History of Consciousness
Neurosutra: The Abhijit Naskar Collection
Autobiography of God: Biopsy of A Cognitive Reality
Biopsy of Religions: Neuroanalysis towards Universal
Tolerance
Prescription: Treating India's Soul
What is Mind?
In Search of Divinity: Journey to The Kingdom of Conscience
Love, God & Neurons: Memoir of a scientist who found
himself by getting lost
The Islamophobic Civilization: Voyage of Acceptance
Neurons of Jesus: Mind of A Teacher, Spouse & Thinker
Neurons, Oxygen & Nanak
The Education Decree
Principia Humanitas
The Krishna Cancer
Rowdy Buddha: The First Sapiens
We Are All Black: A Treatise on Racism
The Bengal Tigress: A Treatise on Gender Equality
Either Civilized or Phobic: A Treatise on Homosexuality
Wise Mating: A Treatise on Monogamy
Illusion of Religion: A Treatise on Religious
Fundamentalism
The Film Testament
Human Making is Our Mission: A Treatise on Parenting
I Am The Thread: My Mission
7 Billion Gods: Humans Above All
Lord is My Sheep: Gospel of Human
Morality Absolute
A Push in Perception
Let The Poor Be Your God
Conscience over Nonsense
Saint of The Sapiens
Time to Save Medicine

Fabric of Humanity
Build Bridges not Walls: In the name of Americana
The Constitution of The United Peoples of Earth
Lives to Serve Before I Sleep
When Humans Unite: Making A World Without Borders
All For Acceptance
Monk Meets World
Mission Reality
Citizens of Peace: Beyond The Savagery of Sovereignty
Operation Justice: To Make A Society That Needs No Law
See No Gender
The Gospel of Technology
Every Generation Needs Caretakers: The Gospel of
Patriotism
Aşkanjali: The Sufi Sermon
Mad About Humans: World Maker's Almanac
Revolution Indomable
When Call The People: My World My Responsibility
No Foreigner Only Family
Hurricane Humans: Give me accountability, I'll give you
peace
Ain't Enough to Look Human
Servitude is Sanctitude
Time To End Democracy: The Meritocratic Manifesto
I Vicdansaadet Speaking: No Rest Till The World is Lifted
Boldly Comes Justice: Sentient not Silent
Good Scientist: When Science and Service Combine
Sleepless for Society
Neden Türk: The Gospel of Secularism
Martyr Meets World: To Solve The Hard Problem of
Inhumanity
The Shape of A Human: Our America Their America
When Veins Ignite: Either Integration or Degradation
Heart Force One: Need No Gun to Defend Society
Solo Standing on Guard: Life Before Law
Generation Corazon: Nationalism is Terrorism
Mucize Insan: When The World is Family
Hometown Human: To Live for Soil and Society
Girl Over God: The Novel (Abi Naskar Adventures Book 1)
Gente Mente Adelante: Prejudice Conquered is World
Conquered
Earthquakin' Egalitarian: I Die Everyday So Your Children
Can Live
Giants in Jeans: 100 Sonnets of United Earth

Vatican Virus: The Forbidden Fiction (Abi Naskar
Adventures Book 2)
Karadeniz Chronicle: The Novel (Abi Naskar Adventures
Book 3)
Şehit Sevda Society: Even in Death I Shall Live
Handcrafted Humanity: 100 Sonnets For A Blunderful
World
Mücadele Muhabbet: Gospel of An Unarmed Soldier
Making Britain Civilized: How to Gain Readmission to The
Human Race
Dervish Advaitam: Gospel of Sacred Feminines and Holy
Fathers
Honor He Wrote: 100 Sonnets For Humans Not Vegetables
The Gentalist: There's No Social Work, Only Family Work
Either Reformist or Terrorist: If You Are Terror I Am Your
Grandfather
Woman Over World: The Novel (Abi Naskar Adventures
Book 4)
High Voltage Habib: Gospel of Undoctrination
Bulldozer on Duty
Find A Cause Outside Yourself: Sermon of Sustainability
Ingan Impossible: Handbook of Hatebusting
Amor Apocalypse: Canım Sana İhtiyacım
Amantes Assemble: 100 Sonnets of Servant Sultans
Mucize Misafir Merhaba: The Peace Testament
Divane Dynamite: Only truth in the cosmos is love
Sin Dios Sí Hay Divinidad: The Pastor Who Never Was

DEDICATION

*This book is dedicated to
the human beings, the real ones.*

CONTENTS

1. Preface: My Mission (The Sonnet).........................1

2. What is Tolerance 5

3. My Revolution (The Sonnet) 9

4. What is Human.........................13

5. Miracle To Be 17

6. Shade (The Sonnet) 21

7. The Answer.........................25

8. Tradition of Barbarism.........................29

9. Backbone Needed 33

10. Prejudice Test.........................37

11. Melanin Maniacs (The Sonnet) 41

12. Whitewashed World (The Sonnet).........................45

13. Citizens of The Future 49

14. Obedience & Oppression.........................55

15. Luxury is Violation.........................59

16. Silicon Psychos (The Sonnet).........................65

17. Code for Humanity (The Sonnet).........................69

18. Stay Behind (The Sonnet) 73

19. Science is Service (The Sonnet).........................77

20. Genius & Conspiracy (The Sonnet) 81

21. AI Con (The Sonnet) 85

22. Evolution & Electronics (The Sonnet) 89

23. Will To Be Civilized.........................93

24.   Revolution & Reform 97

25.   When Education Ruins Harmony 101

26.   Educated on The Streets 105

27.   Education Through Excellence (The Sonnet) ..109

28.   Streets Build Character 113

29.   New Individuality 117

30.   Confusion (A Sonnet).........................121

31.   One Desire (The Sonnet) 125

32.   What is Heart (The Sonnet) 129

33.   Poetry Writes The Poet (The Sonnet)..........133

34.   Enough Analysis (The Sonnet) 137

35.   Practical Mindfulness (The Sonnet)...........141

36.   Sapient Selection (The Sonnet) 145

37.   Corazon Calamidad (The Sonnet) 149

BIBLIOGRAPHY 153

1. Preface: My Mission (The Sonnet)

My Mission
(The Sonnet)

I am not here to inspire butcher doctors,
I am here to build humanitarian doctors.
I am not here to entertain reckless coders,
I am here to invigorate humanitarian coders.
I am not here to arouse mindless engineers,
I am here to torque up humanitarian engineers.
I am not here to pamper crooked politicians,
I am here to wake up the brave world builders.
I am not here to applaud counterfeit philanthropy,
I am here to energize humanitarian entrepreneurs.
I am not here to peddle the glory of logic over life,
I'm here to raise humanitarian scientists 'n philosophers.
There is no rest till humanity courses through human veins.
My mission is to flood the world
with humanitarians by the thousands.

2. What is Tolerance

Siempre adelante,
nunca atrás.
Forever united,
never apart.

When the heart is overrun by hate,
And fervor is f***ed up with phobia,
It's no time for tolerance and truce,
It is time to blow your fuse!

But then again, things are never as black and white as they appear on the surface.

Are they!

So let's clear the air around tolerance right at the beginning.

Let me tell you what my idea of tolerance is, when confronted with inhumanity. In my eyes, even a prehistoric baboon like Donald Dump deserves to live with dignity. If we want the cycle of hate and prejudice to break, we gotta be tolerant of the hateful being, without being tolerant of the hate and prejudice that they practice. If we fail to do so, then how are we any different from those savages!

And this is where the mission of a reformer differs from that of an activist. An activist's mission is to fight the system, a reformer's mission is to reform the system.

In the same way, this is where the mission of a reformer differs from that of a soldier. A soldier's mission is to kill terrorists, a reformer's mission is to end terrorism.

Intolerance deserves no tolerance. But how we stand up to intolerance, that too matters a great deal. The means of revolution is just as significant as revolution itself.

3. My Revolution (The Sonnet)

My Revolution
(The Sonnet)

My revolution has only one golden rule -
No arms, no ideology, only oneness is necessary.
When the heart turns radioactive with compassion,
All war and warheads will become history.

Mi revolución no es la revolución de las pistolas,
Mi revolución es la revolución de la paz y armonía.
Basta ya de la revolución primitiva de las armas,
Somos humanos, nuestra fuerza - espinazo de dinamita.

Enough with revolution of guns and grenades,
It's time to brew the antidote for hate.
All the ingredients can be found in our heart,
We just gotta surpass the ideological barricades.

La gente es mi locura, la gente es mi razón.
Mi corazón insiste, la gente es mi salvación.

4.   What is Human

Remove the ism,
you got race.
Remove the race,
you got the human.
Remove the man,
you got who?
Remove the who,
and you got no clue.
Now we can start,
without any predominance.
Let us discover life,
in its full magnificence.

Life begins where labels end,
World begins where nations end.
Society begins where hate ends,
Peace begins where prejudice ends.

Justice begins where indifference ends,
Community begins where self-centricity ends.
Civilization begins where exclusivity ends,
Mind begins where division ends.

Let everyone hear it, even if they don't get it.

La gente es mi locura,
La gente es mi razón.

Mi corazón insiste,
La gente es mi salvación.

Somos ¡Latino!
¿Sabes lo que significa?
Significa Luz,
Significa Amable,
Significa Tenaz,
Significa Independiente,
Significa No Obediente, No Opresivo.

Obedient to none, oppressive to none -
That's the human way.
Cruel to none, kind to all -
That's the human way.

So to put it simply – we have to decide, whether
we'll remain traditional idiots of inhumanity, or
be the miracle we have the potential to be.

5.   Miracle To Be

A life sectarian is nothing but the ultimate desecration of the miracle that we are. So, instead of carrying on the age-old tradition of desecration, let us use the potential of miracle to do something miraculous - something that our ancestors couldn't even imagine in the wildest of their tribal dreams.

Tribalism is the poison, assimilation is the miracle. Segregation is degradation, integration is ascension. Because, either we integrate, or we disintegrate.

Integration is not an option, integration is fundamental - integration is the evolutionary necessity of a civilized lifeform, whereas the evolutionary necessity of an uncivilized, that is, animal lifeform, is segregation.

The choice is yours - not the choice between life and death, rather the choice between human life and animal life. Living is easy, all the animals do that - living as a human - that takes character.

Every molecule in our body is conditioned through millions of years of natural selection to ensure our survival, but if you can jeopardize your own survival to lift up another life, that, my friend, is called human life.

And any heart that realizes this simple fact of life in their core, es el corazon calamidad - for no injustice, no prejudice, no bias, no inhumanity, stands a chance in front of the gargantuan resolve of such calamitous heart.

By being the calamity to inhumanity, the human heart acts as the gateway to humanity.

Calamitous to inhumanity, serendipitous to humanity - that's the definition of the human heart.

6. Shade (The Sonnet)

22

Shade
(The Sonnet)

Heart is the pedestrian,
Heart is the path.
Heart is the gateway,
Heart is the guard.

Heart is the scenery,
Heart is the sight.
Heart is the land,
Heart is the light.

Heart is the discoverer,
Heart is discovery.
Heart is the worshipper,
Heart is almighty.

There's nothing more tragic than a heart all folded.
Heart alone is the seed, heart alone is the shade.

7. The Answer

We talked plenty about the human heart, so here one wonders - what is the role of the head then, if any?

To which I say, it's not that complicated really, even though the head has a tendency to complicate things.

It is this simple. Heart shows the way, head provides the means.

However, in practice head doesn't really work as a separate agency, rather it integrates with the heart and amplifies the heart's capacity - all of which anatomically takes place within the brain.

Somos la pregunta, somos la respuesta. We are the question, we are the answer.

And what is that answer?

What is that ultimate answer to all the troubles of our world?

That answer - that supreme solution to all pollution, is accountability - everyday, ordinary, civilian accountability, independent of policy, independent of law, independent of science, as well as religion.

When politicians go astray, accountability is the answer. When intellectuals go astray, accountability is the answer. When the elites go astray, accountability is the answer.

When the civilians remember their responsibility, politicians will forget which party they belong to, so will their next of kin. And at the slightest urge for exploitation, a voice of caution will ring in their head - don't you dare, kid - or else, you'll have neither the seat nor the ass to sit on it!

Now the question rises. Aren't the politicians also civilians? Aren't the intellectuals also civilians? Aren't the elites also civilians?

In theory - yes!

But in practice, they behave anything but civilian. In practice, they behave like self-appointed monarchs of the world.

And it's not really their fault. That's what history has taught us all about how the world works.

8. Tradition of Barbarism

You see, there is no such thing as world history. Almost everything you read in school about history is propaganda. It's the propaganda of the oppressors sold to produce new oppressors and new oppressed. And don't tell me this is not true, when the very paradigm of education is founded, not on excellence, but on competition.

I mean, take Britain for example. How can a civilized people be so dumb, backward and practically savage as to still maintain some prehistoric tradition of declaring certain individuals ruler of a land based on bloodline!

Grow up, already!

Barbarism, thy name is Britain. In this day and age, if any societal structure is a revolting blot on the fabric of the democratic world, it's not Russia or North Korea, but the not-so-great Britain. Pretend democracy is worse than straightforward dictatorship.

The queen might have been a nice person, I don't know. But when a person is declared the supreme authority (head of state) of an entire people by birth, it's not something to take pride in, rather it's something to be ashamed of.

Britain may mourn the death of the queen as a person, but no land deserves to be called civilized while mourning the death of a monarch. Let me put this into perspective. Almost every week a country celebrates independence from britain - if this doesn't tell you why the monarchy is the antithesis of everything that is civilized, nothing can.

I wonder, they can throw a homeless man in jail for lifting a bread out of hunger, yet the empire walks free, even after raping, pillaging and looting from 90% of the world's countries!

Where is the ICC (International Criminal Court) now, when one monarch after another sits on the throne, wielding the crown jewels encrusted with national treasures stolen from all over the globe!

9. Backbone Needed

I have no beef with those brits who have realized the fallacies of monarchy - in fact, these are the only civilized beings in britain. So when I use the terms savage and backward, I am referring to the monarchy enthusiasts.

The point is, when the descendants of a brutish empire continue to represent and maintain the authority of that empire, such descendants do not deserve even an ounce of respect from civilized humans, any more than their ancestors do, let alone be declared head of state. It'd be like respecting a neonazi for advocating for a new confederate America.

Until a society develops the backbone to strip every single monarch of their throne, palace and power, and turns them into a commoner, such society is nothing but a clinically medieval stain upon the fabric of a civilized world.

If we are to ever become civilized, then we must stand ready to discard anything and everything that stands as impediment to equality and egalitarianism – including our most revered customs and traditions.

No matter what worked in the past - we must stop measuring our life based on the standards concocted by our shortsighted ancestors. We must write our own measures.

We must grab hold of our prejudices and dump them in the trash, along with every last trace of tradition that endorses hate and division. And for that, we gotta be aware - we gotta be aware of ourselves - ten times more aware than our ancestors ever were in their wildest dreams.

10. Prejudice Test

You say, you don't have any prejudice! Let's put that to test, shall we! Read the following phrases, pausing a few seconds after each.

Hallelujah!

¡Viva la libertad!

Shabbat Shalom!

Allahu Akbar!

Black Lives Matter!

We're Here, We're Queer!

My body, my decision!

Now bring your faculty of reason into action, and think, which of the terms induced a negative emotional response in your mind? It's nothing out of the ordinary, it's just common animal nature.

How your brain got conditioned to react in such a way that's a different matter. The main thing is, your brain just reacted exactly like the brain of pavlov's dog every time it heard the bell. The only difference is that, a dog doesn't have further brain capacity to question such conditioning, but a human does.

Which means that, if we do not have the courage and conscience to question our prejudices and biases, then we don't deserve to be called human.

I'll say it to you plainly. An animal becomes human by self-correction, not by glorifying their animality as tradition.

Such act of humanity may enrage those who take pride in their primitivity, but you mustn't let their hate infect you.

Let me give you an example.

Bigots have a name for me - Abhishit Nutscar. Which is actually quite flattering to me, because in sanskrit "abhi" means fearless. So all I hear is, "wounded nutter with some fearless shit". Love you, kids! Get well, soon!

11. Melanin Maniacs
(The Sonnet)

Melanin Maniacs
(The Sonnet)

White guy writes a couple of sonnets and plays,
And he is idolized as an olympian deity.
Colored guy smashes the paradigm to ashes,
And it warrants absolute unacceptability.
Apparently, greatness is only greatness,
If it can be credited to a caucasian.
Otherwise they only end up pondering,
What's the deal with this non-white person!
It's a sad, sad world we live in,
All the advancement is on the outside.
Inside we are dumber than Donald Duck,
Which has ruined all hope for real insight.
Enough of this obsession with white aphrodisiacs!
It's time to act as humans, and not melanin maniacs.

Note: Let me tell you a secret which everybody knows but nobody will admit. In this world everything is ten times less difficult, if you are white.

44

12. Whitewashed World
(The Sonnet)

Whitewashed World
(The Sonnet)

I once sent my sonnets for an official recognition,
They rejected me saying, I lack skill and significance.
It's a white people's world after all, like it or not,
We wouldn't want the little white poets to take offence!
My skin doesn't radiate the glory of talcum powder,
So I'm supposed to be thankful for the white hand-me-downs.
Mine is not to seek recognition in a whitewashed world,
Mine is to keep on struggling with my vigor's last ounce.
In a world where top white export is but oppression,
Everything is ten times less difficult if you are white.
A mermaid of color tickles the conquerors the wrong way,
White people's Nobel disproportionately goes to the whites.
Whether you recognize me or not, I neither care nor mind.
The reason I write this, so humankind becomes human and kind.

13. Citizens of The Future

Hate, prejudice and discrimination don't disappear merely by refraining from using certain terms out of political correctness. We gotta get to the root of these vicious violations of human rights, and dismantle them from their core - only then shall we witness the dawn of a truly just and democratic civilization.

We gotta treat the cause, not the symptom. We gotta treat the hate, and divisions will disappear on their own. We gotta bring down the barriers, and bridges will appear out of nowhere.

Let me put this into perspective.

Having a multicultural existence, for each work my mind by nature leans towards a particular culture that serves best as the backbone of that particular work. Because of which people often ask me, how can one person speak as family on behalf of so many cultures, without any prejudice!

I tell them, I don't know how to do it any other way.

You see, once you bring down the barriers in your mind, universal belonging comes naturally.

When I was a nobody I only knew one thing. If I was to raise citizens of the future, free from the petty nationalistic squabbles and cultural divisions, whose nationality would be humanity, religion love, and culture compassion, I had to be the first anomalous example of such sectlessness myself.

So I became one.

My very life is a revolt against division and discrimination. Correction - civilized human life ought to be a roaring revolt against division and discrimination. Human life ought to be an uproar against every heinous force that is divisive and discriminatory in this world.

Or else, it is no civilized life to begin with.

Or else, it is no human life to begin with.

Because civilization is another name for undivision.

Humanity is another name for oneness.

Humanidad es unidad.

I am not talkin' about rejecting your roots. I am simply askin' you to expand on your roots.

Why?

Because, expansion is life, whereas stagnation is death.

14. Obedience & Oppression

Do away with stagnation once and for all. Don't let nobody tell you that that very stagnation is your identity. Remember, those who teach stagnation as identity never came to life in the first place to teach anybody anything.

Teaching is an act of life, and those who peddle stagnation, are peddling death, not life. So, leave them to their deadly delusions if they so please, but don't take them as authority in your life. Their delusion is their choice, don't make it yours.

In fact, as I said in the ten humanitarian commandments, don't take nobody as authority in your life.

I repeat, you are your authority, period.

But be very cautious - this is not an affirmation of egotism. Being your own authority doesn't mean you are free to do whatever you like, whenever you like - it simply means, you are obedient to nobody, just like you ought to be oppressive to nobody, either directly or through plain recklessness.

Egotism is nothing but a kind of oppression, for it is an act of condescension. It is an act of living in a prehistoric bubble of supremacy, not unlike our bigoted and divided ancestors. Whether you are slave to others or to yourself, it's still slavery - which is the very habit we oughta be cautious against.

Let me give you an example. There is a difference between the pursuit of life essentials and the pursuit of luxury. Yet we live in a world where the very line is nonexistent. And that's how disparity is born. Then we foolishly wonder, how can we treat the disparities of society!

15. Luxury is Violation

A world that confuses luxury with success, has absolutely zero understanding of the human condition. That's why they idolize rich and filthy celebrities with private jets and rolls royce, as some sort of demigods. If this is your idea of success, then you guys are more disgustingly primitive than the wildlife in the amazon. At least, wild animals don't pretend to be civilized.

And while we are on the topic of luxury, let me point out one more thing. It's high time we put some humanity into the mess which we call an economic paradigm - that not only glorifies the practice of luxury - but what's more important is that, it rather shamelessly paves the way for such luxury.

It is time we rid the economy of its ridiculous disparities, by axing the revolting salary gap in various industries. A CEO shouldn't get several hundred times the salary that the janitor is paid. An athlete shouldn't get several hundred times the salary that the waterboy is paid. A filmstar shouldn't get several hundred times the salary that the crew at the bottom are paid.

I understand if you are not yet civilized enough to flatten the field completely – for you are an infantile species after all. But at the very least, do your best to reduce the gap - that is, if you intend to be human someday.

The glory may differ based on the kind of work a person does, but nobody should suffer to make ends meet while others fly in private jets. Economic growth doesn't mean the growth of disparity, it means the end of disparity. And we can never end disparity from our society unless we cut off all ties with luxury, preferably by individual accountability, if not, then by means of policy.

Riches maketh filth, filth pursue riches. To live a life of luxury, or to dream of a life of luxury, doesn't make us ambitious, it only exposes the moron that we are. A species that has not realized simplicity as the way of life, will never in a million years have a society without disease and disparity.

I won't mince my words, and tell you straight. Wanna be a decent human being? Stay away from luxury. Because luxury is a violation of human rights, human health, and above all, human character.

It's funny really! Some people can't afford two wholesome meals a day, while others live with a private airport in their backyard. Some parents work their butt off to keep the clothes on their children's back, while others shower their kids with lamborghinis and teslas. If this doesn't open your eyes, perhaps you should try lobotomy. I'm sure you can find some unlicensed surgeon somewhere who'd do it for you if you offer them a trip to the bahamas, or better yet, a trip to space in your own spaceship.

The human point is - there is a difference between science that serves the society, and science that serves oligarchic craving for authority. Until we learn the difference between the two, all science is superstition.

Science is sacred. Use it wisely. Remember, worse than the absence of science, is the abuse of science.

What is Science? Science means Sapient Conscientious Investigation of Eternity with No Compromise on Empathy.

Let put it into perspective. Better have no science, than a science used for inhuman purposes. Better have no civilization than one that is civilized only on the outside.

16. Silicon Psychos
(The Sonnet)

Silicon Psychos
(The Sonnet)

If we cared more about the hard problem of real inhumanity,
And less about the fictitious hard problem of consciousness,
We'd have filled the world with human consciousness already,
Instead of still fighting for basic rights against base biases.
What kind of a moron goes walkabout when their home is on fire,
What kind of a moron abandons the living chasing life on silicon!
We really gotta take a hard look at our habits and priorities,
Dreaming is good, but dream devoid of life is but degeneration.
Chimps driving teslas are still chimps no matter the demagoguery,
All intelligence is disgrace if it's unaware of human condition.
A heartless organism living on silicon is no different,
From a heartless organism living in a carbon based human.
Be it crucifix or code, in savage hands every tool is weapon.
The wise use AI to design prosthetics, savages for transhumanism.

17. Code for Humanity
(The Sonnet)

Code for Humanity
(The Sonnet)

There is no such thing as ethical hacking,
If it were ethical they wouldn't be teaching it.
Because like it or not ethics is bad for business,
They teach hacking so they could use it for profit.
With the right sequence of zeros and ones we could,
Equalize all bank accounts of planet earth tomorrow.
Forget about what glass house gargoyles do with tech,
How will you the human use tech to eliminate sorrow?
In a world full of greedy edisons, be a humble Tesla,
Time remembers no oligarch kindly no matter the status.
Only innovators who get engraved in people's heart,
Are the ones who innovate with a humane purpose.
Innovate to bridge the gap, not exploit and cater to disparities.
In a world run by algorithms of greed write a code
that helps 'n heals.

18. Stay Behind (The Sonnet)

Stay Behind
(The Sonnet)

While mine owners' kids are packing,
Their mittens to colonize Mars,
How about you stay behind,
To give light as an earthly human star!
I am not here to teach you how to code,
I am here to show you why code.
I am not here to teach you science,
But to humanize the scientific road.
Okay if they don't know the role of science,
You for one, don't walk in their dirtsteps.
You are wise, brave, and above all, human,
Be the practitioner of humanitarian science.
Science is superpower, always use it wisely.
Little science does much harm if used recklessly.

19. Science is Service
(The Sonnet)

Science is Service
(The Sonnet)

Extraordinary technology brings extraordinary recklessness,
Because the human mind hasn't matured like technology has.
We may have developed technology that defies human limits,
Evolutionary predispositions of the mind haven't disappeared.
That's why I say, bigger the power the smaller the mind.
For a wielder without backbone, silicon is but plaything.
Even an ounce of science can do unimaginable harm.
To fathom it you gotta step out of the glare most blinding.
Science 'n society go together, can't have one without the other.
Where there is love for science, there is love for society.
If this simple thing doesn't penetrate the skull of us thickies.
We would be better off without all the scientific glory.
Science is an act of service in the course of lifting all humanity.
Science without accountability is no different
from a conspiracy theory.

20. Genius & Conspiracy
(The Sonnet)

Genius & Conspiracy
(The Sonnet)

Wherever there is extraordinary genius,
There are extraordinary conspiracy theories.
Because the human mind cannot distinguish,
Supernatural mysticism from natural mysteries.
Wherever there is exceptional talent,
There is talk of divine intervention.
Because the mind cannot fathom excellence,
Without involving some good old mystification.
We may tolerate some conspiracies that are innocent,
But those that do harm are human rights violation.
If we can't use it when we need to use it the most,
What's the point in carrying around a lofty brain!
There are times when reason must take a back seat,
Then there're times, ignorance mustn't be given heed.

21. AI Con (The Sonnet)

AI Con
(The Sonnet)

Everybody is concerned about psychics conning people,
How 'bout the billionaires who con people using science!
Con artists come in all shapes and sizes,
Some use barnum statements, others artificial intelligence.
Most scientists speak up against only the little frauds,
But not the big frauds who support their livelihood.
Am I not afraid to be blacklisted by the big algorithms!
Is the sun afraid, its light will offend some puny hoods!
I come from the soil, I'll die struggling in the soil.
My needs are less, hence my integrity is dangerous.
I am here to show this infantile species how to grow up.
I can't be bothered by the fragility of a few spoiled brats.
Reason and fiction both are fundamental to build a civilization.
Neither is the problem, the problem is greed and self-absorption.

22. Evolution & Electronics
(The Sonnet)

Evolution & Electronics
(The Sonnet)

I know electronic circuitry like the back of my hand,
Yet it's the human mind that fascinates me most immensely.
Fascination in electronics lies in new design possibility,
Whereas the mind is the breeding ground of all possibility.
Our engineering is puny compared to that of Mother Nature,
Each day a new mystery unfolds in the vast organic kingdom.
Our puny electronics work based on cold 'n rigid computation,
Evolution of life in nature is predicated on plastic mutation.
That's why we must never disregard nature blinded by arrogance,
We may have conquered nature's mercy but we're still subordinate.
The moment a lifeform starts to vilify the womb whence it came,
With a single blow creator nature can flatten all our obstinance.
Foster humility and wisdom, before going nuts about technology.
Don't end up yet another fancy stain upon the honor of humanity.

23. Will To Be Civilized

94

Civilization starts with accountability. And accountability comes naturally when the entire world becomes your family - when you start to feel restless unless you wipe some tears and cause some cheer. This is civilization in practice, free from intellect, free from philosophy, free from the petty bickering of a primitive species.

The fact of the matter is, a true civilization needs no philosophy or intellect or religion to be civilized. It is only when we have no real desire to be civilized that we beat around the bush with arguments of philosophy and religion.

Which means that, if you have the will to be civilized, you'll act civilized with or without Naskar, with or without Chomsky, with or without Socrates - but if you have no such real intention to begin with, then even a hundred Naskars, Socrates' and Chomskys won't be able to inject civilization into your dampened veins.

External agencies can help, but only if there is some intention on your part. External agencies can help, only after you've realized your responsibility towards the world - only after you've realized your responsibility as a civilized human being.

There is no civilization outside, unless there is civilization inside. There is no justice outside, unless there is justice inside. There is no equality outside, unless there is equality inside. There is no humanity outside, unless there is humanity inside.

It is this simple.

You are the revolution that you are waiting for. You are the revolution that the world desperately needs.

24. Revolution & Reform

When we speak of revolution, we usually associate it with a lot of people protesting on the streets. I am not talking about that kind of revolution, at least not here anyway. I am talking about being the revolution in your everyday walk of life.

I am talking about an everyday revolution against the everyday inhumanities, that we often walk away from, because we don't wanna be involved, lest we get in trouble.

That's the kind of revolution this world needs - not some big revolution where once in a while people in large numbers come together to protest against a big injustice, but small everyday revolutions where the individual refuses to submit to the small injustices that they come across in their daily life.

That's how we reform a planet, not by occasional acts of big revolution, but through regular practice of small reformation. Big revolution changes party, small everyday revolution changes paradigm.

Anybody can walk amidst a hundred protestors, but to walk alone daily on the path of humanity amidst inhumanity - that takes backbone. Here I am not dissing the big revolutionary protests, rather what I am pointing out is that, we mustn't glorify the big revolutions over and above individual accountability in everyday life.

The point is, if you have to see hundreds of people come to the streets against an injustice, in order to realize that it is an injustice, then I'm afraid such injustice will continue to haunt our society in one form or another till kingdom come.

Collective revolt only postpones injustice, whereas individual accountability cures injustice.

25. When Education Ruins Harmony

The problem is that the architecture of our very society is founded on the fundamental act of unaccountability, that is, indifference. Take the world's method of education for example.

Schools don't teach accountability to the kids, they teach competition. Competition is the backbone of education, not accountability, let alone character or wisdom. And with competition as the lifeblood of education, how can we ever expect to raise citizens with inclinations of harmony and peace!

With competition as backbone, how can we ever expect the citizens of tomorrow to be driven by a sense of curiosity in the course of collective uplift, rather than being driven by superstition and selfishness!

As a result, even though education is theoretically the foundation of academia, more often than less the most astounding beacons of education, or rather I should say, the torchbearers of true knowledge, come from outside academia.

But why?

Why do so many mental giants come from outside academia?

My particular favorite on this matter is Srinivasa Ramanujan.

Anyway, the answer is actually simpler than it looks. It's just that education is a dynamic force, but the moment you stuff that force behind walls, in an attempt to mechanize it, you inadvertently end up eliminating its naively dynamic freedom of expression that made it so potent a force in the first place.

Don't get me wrong, academia has its place, but don't make the mistake of thinking that academia as we have today is the ultimate cradle of education. Academia is merely a vessel, and a rather mighty vessel at that, but it is the human mind that is the almighty source of all education.

Remember, education is supposed to reform the world, not ruin it.

26. Educated on The Streets

Even though I was never academically trained in scientific reasoning, reasoning comes to me like breathing. In the same way, even though I was never academically trained in philosophy and poetry, they come to me like walking in the park.

To put it simply, academia contributed very little in the making of Naskar. Heck, the only reason I trudged through a couple of semesters of engineering even after being disillusioned with the prehistoric pedagogy, was so I could sit at the backbenches and pay my silent homage to a girl at the front bench with my eyes.

Then when she rejected me, I dropped out and started roaming the streets as a vagabond, quite literally. And that's where my real education began - amidst the dust and dirt of the streets. Streets taught me science, streets taught me religion, streets taught me poetry. But more importantly, it's the streets that turned a nobody into a champion for those struggling on the streets everywhere in the world.

That's why today, even though I walk amongst some of the fanciest people on earth due to my work as a brain and behavior expert, I still feel somewhat alien. As I once said, I prefer to sit on the sidewalk and share a hotdog with a homeless person, than dine with a world leader at some fancy restaurant.

But the question is, is it really I, who is the alien here? Or is it those people who are so cold and phony to their bones that one has to prepare for a trip to the arctic before meeting them!

I don't know the answer.

Do you?

They call it professionalism, I call it the desecration of life.

I'll put it to you straight. If you take away warmth from the world, what do you have left?

A freezer, which is home for the dead, not the living.

27. Education Through Excellence
(The Sonnet)

Education Through Excellence
(The Sonnet)

During my aimless years I once had an urge,
To learn about jet propulsion engine.
So I wrote content for tech support websites,
To buy a couple of books on aeronautics.
Education means catering to curiosity,
Study to gain excellence not a certificate.
If it doesn't open your eyes to social ascension,
Education only causes the world to dehydrate.
You can stuff entire encyclopedias into your head,
That still will not make you an educated being.
If education was the same thing as information,
Google would be the omniscient superbeing.
Certificate without humanity is a ticket to stoneage.
If it takes away your warmth, it is all decadence.

28. Streets Build Character

Whatever you do, and however high you fly, never lose your warmth, my friend - never lose your touch with the streets - with the soil. And I am not saying this only to those who practically come from the streets and the soil, but to everybody.

If you come from the streets and the soil, never lose your touch with 'em, and if you don't come from the streets and the soil, that is, if you are born into privilege, then it is your duty as a civilized human being to step across your privilege, and foster a connection of the heart with the streets and the soil.

Your family background is of no importance to your identity as a human being. Your identity is your character. And the only place where character is built is on the streets and the soil, that is, amidst struggle, amidst humility, amidst the warmth of everyday humanity.

Be the character that the world never dares to develop. Be esperanza impossible - be the hope impossible, that the world is too insecure to foster. Turn your very existence into a walking declaration of life, light and liberty, against all the predominant insecurity, indifference and inhumanity.

I repeat, it is not about big revolts and big wins, it's about not turning a blind eye to those little everyday inhumanities that you encounter in daily life. You are the revolution - you, the individual - not the crowd.

29. New Individuality

Don't rely on anybody to join your struggle for justice and equality - it's your struggle, yours alone! Unless you muster the mettle to go against the most menacing monstrosity in your society all on your own, this world of ours will never foster a sentience without all the sickening psychosis of sectarianism, selfishness and superstition.

Till every individual turns into a walking revolution against bigotry, prejudice, discrimination and dehumanization, without relying on others, discrimination and dehumanization will never end - they'll merely change shape in the face of occasional outrage from the crowd, but they'll never truly end.

Only the individual can end inhumanity, not the crowd. Only the individual can end inhumanity, not the law. Only the individual can end inhumanity, not the government.

That is why I say, individuality doesn't mean individual identity, individuality means individual accountability. Accountability is your identity - you the human that is. And if there is no accountability in the individual, every other quality of the individual isn't worth a burnt cigarette butt.

You don't need guns for that, you don't bombs for that, you don't even need hands and feet for that matter. All you need is a heart - a heart that boils and a heart that toils.

In a world run by septicemia, be the antiseptic. Shine your antiseptic light so bright, that all the bigots, racists, nationalists, supremacists and dollarists start to itch all over.

30. Confusion (A Sonnet)

Confusion
(The Sonnet)

Society that confuses competition with education,
Has no idea what knowledge or education is.
Society that confuses memorizing with learning,
Has no idea what learning for wisdom really means.
Society that confuses guns with gallantry,
Has no idea what gallantry is.
Society that tries for peace with bombs,
Earns more contracts for bombs not peace.
Society that confuses luxury with success,
Never gets the civilized sense of success.
Society that confuses materials with happiness,
Keeps drowning in materials away from happiness.
A life well lived is a life lived amidst people.
Any system that creates divide belongs in the jungle.

31. One Desire (The Sonnet)

One Desire
(The Sonnet)

I speak most, when I speak nothing,
Light unfolds only in the dark.
Listen to my words, you'll hear my head,
Listen to my silence, you'll hear my heart.
Upon pouring out an insurmountable universe,
Of words into the world, I have but one desire.
I just wanna sit next to someone and say nothing,
While they gently put their head on my shoulder.
Don't know when I'll ever have my long awaited rest,
When I'll have to explain nothing to no one!
Don't get me wrong, I cherish my work greatly but,
There's plenty I never got to cherish with someone.
This is me being human shedding light on human condition.
Even the giant isn't impregnable to life's sweet expectation.

32. What is Heart (The Sonnet)

What is Heart
(The Sonnet)

The heart wants what the heart wants,
But not always what the heart wants is human.
There's a lot of ways the term heart unfolds,
Sometimes it shelters love, sometimes division.
It is not enough to associate heart with emotions,
It is time we associate heart with wholeness.
Some emotions are expression of sheer prejudice,
Hence, reason must be a part of heart's wholeness.
We often boast a separation between thought 'n emotion,
In reality, it's impossible to tell thought from emotion.
The important thing is not to tell thought from emotion,
But to not behave a savage, be it in thought or emotion.
Human being is whole being, whole being is human being.
If there is no wholeness, we're just a bunch of dumplings.

33. Poetry Writes The Poet
(The Sonnet)

134

Poetry Writes The Poet
(The Sonnet)

The best poets are the ones,
Who don't know how to write poetry.
Just like the best scientists are those,
Who practice science as everyday curiosity.
The more you focus on the definition,
The more you lose touch with the essence.
That is why I never know what my work is about,
To explain love is to lose love's fragrance.
Painting of a landscape is not the landscape itself,
Depiction must never be confused with the depicted.
I don't know how to do small talk, hence the sonnets.
Poet doesn't write poetry, poetry writes the poet.
The moment I think I am in control, I lose all control.
Craving no control, the river just nourishes the soul.

34. Enough Analysis
(The Sonnet)

Enough Analysis
(The Sonnet)

Poet knows no poetry,
Sage knows no wisdom.
Lover can't explain love,
Saint can't explain undivision.
Explanation is an act of analysis,
Explanation warrants a lot of division.
Facts and figures can be quantified,
But the mind is beyond computation.
Human is home to the human,
What is there to analyze!
Problem is that we analyze plenty,
But in times of need very little we realize.
When someone's world is crumbling down into abyss,
Practice humanity instead of practicing analysis.

140

35. Practical Mindfulness
(The Sonnet)

Practical Mindfulness
(The Sonnet)

When someone's world is crumbling down,
Reach out to lend a shoulder not analysis.
If the world had more carers and sharers,
We wouldn't need the services of therapists.
Most humans are raised to be selfish robots,
Then they spend their life on a therapist's sofa.
When someone's going through a period of grief,
Only the mindless comments, 'have you tried yoga!'
For the human mind to be whole and healthy,
You gotta empty it of all the unhealthy junk.
And there is no greater junk on the face of earth,
Than the traditions that make us self-centric drunk.
Elimination of coldness is the highest of all wisdom.
Treat the common cold, and you'll treat all descension.

36. Sapient Selection
(The Sonnet)

Sapient Selection
(The Sonnet)

Some people engineer machines,
I engineer human evolution.
How can we engineer evolution,
Simply by taking accountable action.
This is what I call sapient selection,
When humans choose the path they take.
Sure, nature still has a huge hold over us but,
We have the neurons to override her influence.
It is extremely difficult to conquer nature,
But the important thing is, it is not impossible.
With enough resolve, honor and conscience,
Anybody can tame their inner animal.
Monkeys that walk upright are still monkeys.
Sapiens with hate are but good-looking chimpanzees.

37. Corazon Calamidad
(The Sonnet)

Corazon Calamidad
(The Sonnet)

A society that doesn't know the difference,
Between a good-looking chimp and sapiens,
May travel to alpha centauri for all I care,
But will still remain a lifeform of decadence.
If we placed half as much attention,
On the inside as we place on the outside,
We'd be living by now on a planet called earth,
Instead of a graveyard of prejudice and fright.
God's will is whatever the human wills,
Upon your will depends the course of human evolution.
Or you could just lean back and watch the game while,
Intellectual degenerates drag us all into degeneration.
Earth needs no humanity, but ain't no humano sin humanidad.
To build a world suitable for humans,
each heart must stand on guard as corazon calamidad.

BIBLIOGRAPHY

154

Archer M., (2000), Being Human: The Problem of Agency. Cambridge University Press.

Adolphs R (2003) Cognitive neuroscience of human social behaviour. Nature Rev Neurosci 4: 165–178.

Adolphs R, Tranel D, Damasio AR (2003) Dissociable neural systems for recognizing emotions. Brain Cogn 52: 61–69.

Andresen, Jensine, and Robert Forman, eds. Cognitive Models and Spiritual Maps. Bowling Green, Ohio: Imprint Academic, 2000.

Azari, Nina, Janpeter Nickel, Gilbert Wunderlich, Michael Niedeggen, Harald Hefter, Lutz Tellmann, Hans Herzog, Petra Stoerig, Dieter Birnbacher, and Rudiger Seitz. "Neural

Correlates of Religious Experience." European Journal of Neuroscience 13, no. 8 (2001)

Agar, N. (2004). Liberal eugenics: In defence of human enhancement. London: Blackwell Publishing.

Alteheld, N., Roessler, G., Vobig, M., & Walter, R. (2004). The retina implant new approach to a visual prosthesis. Biomedizinische Technik, 49(4), 99–103.

Antal, A., Nitsche, M. A., Kincses, T. Z., Kruse, W., Hoffmann, K. P., & Paulus, W. (2004a). Facilitation of visuo-motor learning by transcranial direct current stimulation of the motor and extrastriate visual areas in humans. European Journal of Neuroscience, 19(10), 2888–2892.

Bernstein R.J., (1971), Praxis and Action: Contemporary Philosophies of Human Activity. Philadelphia: University of Pennsylvania Press.

Bernstein R.J., (1976), The Restructuring Social and Political Thought.

Bernstein R.J., (1983), Beyond Relativism and Objectivism: Science, Hermeneutics, and Praxis. Philadelphia: University of Pennsylvania Press.

Bernstein R.J., (1986), Philosophical Profiles. Philadelphia: University of Pennsylvania Press.

Bernstein R.J., (1991), New Constellation. Cambridge: MIT Press.

Birkhead, T. R., Johnson, S. D. & Nettleship, D. N. (1985). Extra-pair matings and mate guarding in the common murre Uria aalge. - Anim. Behav. 33, p. 608-619.

Beauregard, Mario, and Vincent Paquette. "Neural Correlates of a Mystical Experience in Carmelite Nuns." Neuroscience Letters 405, no. 3 (2006)

Benson, Herbert. Timeless Healing: The Power and Biology of Belief. New York: Scribner, 1996

Bose, Subhas Chandra. An Indian Pilgrim: An Unfinished Autobiography, Oxford University Press, 1997

Bogen, J.E.(1995a), 'On the neurophysiology of consciousness: Part I. An overview', Consciousness and Cognition, 4.

Bogen, J.E. (1995b), 'On the neurophysiology of consciousness: Part II. Constraining the semantic problem', Consciousness and Cognition, 4.

Bremner, J. D., R. Soufer, et al. (2001). "Gender differences in cognitive and neural correlates of remembrance of emotional words." Psychopharmacol Bull 35 (3).

Brothers, L. (2002). The social brain: A project for integrating primate behavior and neurophysiology in a new domain. In J. T. Cacioppo et al. (Eds.), Foundations in neuroscience. Cambridge, MA: MIT Press.

Buss, D. D. (2003). Evolutionary Psychology: The New Science of Mind, 2nd ed. New York: Allyn & Bacon.

Buss, D. M. (1989). "Conflict between the sexes: Strategic interference and the evocation of anger and upset." J Pers Soc Psychol 56 (5).

Buss, D. M. (1995). "Psychological sex differences. Origins through sexual selection." Am Psychol 50 (3).

Buss, D. M., and D. P. Schmitt (1993). "Sexual strategies theory: An evolutionary perspective on human mating." Psychol Rev 100 (2).

Blakemore SJ, Decety J (2001) From the perception of action to the understanding of intention. Nature Rev Neurosci 2: 561.

Colapietro V., (1988), "Human Agency: The Habits of Our Being." Southern Journal of Philosophy, XXVI, 2, pp. 153-68.

Colapietro V., (1992), "Purpose, Power, and Agency." The Monist, 75, 4 (October) pp. 423-44.

Colapietro V., (2004a), "C. S. Peirce's Reclamation of Teleology." Nature in American Philosophy, ed. Jean De Groot (Washington, D.C.: Catholic University Press of America), pp. 88-108.

Carey DP, Perrett DI, Oram MW (1997) Recognizing, understanding and reproducing actions. In: Jeannerod M, Grafman J (eds) Handbook of neuropsychology. Vol. 11: Action and cognition. Elsevier, Amsterdam.

Carr L, Iacoboni M, Dubeau MC, Mazziotta JC, Lenzi GL (2003) Neural mechanisms of empathy in humans: a relay from neural systems for imitation to limbic areas. Proc Natl Acad Sci USA 100: 5497–5502.

Chomsky Noam, (2017) Requiem for the American Dream

Chomsky Noam, (2016) Who Rules the World?

Chomsky Noam, (2010) How the World Works

Churchland, P.S. (1986), Neurophilosophy (Cambridge, MA: The MIT Press).

Churchland, P.S. & Ramachandran, V.S. (1993), 'Filling in: Why Dennett is wrong', in Dennett and His Critics: Demystifying Mind, ed. B. Dahlbom (Oxford: Blackwell Scientific Press).

Churchland, P.S., Ramachandran, V.S. & Sejnowski, T.J. (1994), 'A critique of pure vision', in Large- scale Neuronal Theories of the Brain, ed. C. Koch & J.L. Davis (Cambridge, MA: The MIT Press).

Coyle EF. Integration of the physiological factors determining endurance performance ability. Exerc Sport Sci Rev. 1995;23:25–63.

Crick, F. (1994), The Astonishing Hypothesis: The Scientific Search for the Soul (New York: Simon and Schuster).

Crick, F. (1996), 'Visual perception: rivalry and consciousness', Nature, 379.

Crick, F. & Koch, C. (1992), 'The problem of consciousness', Scientific American, 267.

Damasio, A (2003a) Looking for Spinoza. Harcourt Inc. Damasio A (2003b) Feeling of emotion and the self. Ann NY Acad Sci 1001: 253–261.

d'Aquili, Eugene. "Senses of Reality in Science and Religion." Zygon 17, no 4 (1982)

d'Aquili, Eugene. "The Biopsychological Determinants of Religious Ritual Behavior." Zygon 10, no. 1 (1975)

d'Aquili, Eugene. "The Myth-Ritual Complex: A Biogenetic Structural Analysis." Zygon 18, no. 3 (1983)

d'Aquili, Eugene, and Andrew Newberg. The Mystical Mind: Probing the Biology of Religious Experience. Minneapolis: Fortress Press, 1999.

Daly DD. 1958. Ictal affect. Am J Psychiatry.

Damasio, A. (1994) Descartes' Error: Emotion, Reason and the Human Brain. New York, Putnams.

Damasio, A. (1999) The Feeling of What Happens: Body, Emotion and the Making of Consciousness. London, Heinemann.

Darwin, C. (1859) On the Origin of Species by Means of Natural Selection. London, Murray.

Darwin, C. (1871) The Descent of Man and Selection in Relation to Sex. London, John Murray.

Darwin, C. (1872) The Expression of the Emotions in Man and Animals. London, John Murray; also published 1965, Chicago, University of Chicago Press.

Dawkins, M.S. (1987) Minding and mattering. In C. Blakemore and S. Greenfield (eds) Mindwaves. Oxford, Blackwell, 151-60.

Dawkins, R. (1976) The Selfish Gene. Oxford, Oxford University Press; a new edition, with additional material, was published in 1989.

Di Pellegrino G, Fadiga L, Fogassi L, Gallese V, Rizzolatti G (1992) Understanding motor events: A neurophysiological study. Exp Brain Res 91: 176–80.

Deikman, A.J. (2000) A functional approach to mysticism. Journal of Consciousness Studies 7(11-12), 75-91.

Delmonte, M.M. (1987) Personality and meditation. In M. West (ed.) The Psychology of Meditation. Oxford, Clarendon Press, 118-32.

Dennett, D.C. (1988) Quining qualia. In A.J. Marcel and E. Bisiach (eds) Consciousness in Contemporary Science. Oxford, Oxford University Press, 42-77.

Dennett, D.C. (1991) Consciousness Explained. Boston, MA, and London, Little, Brown and Co.

Dennett, D.C. (1995a) Darwin's Dangerous Idea. London, Penguin.

Dennett, D.C. (1998b) Brainchildren: Essays on Designing Minds. Cambridge, MA, MIT Press.

Dewhurst, Kenneth, and A. W. Beard. "Sudden Religious Conversions in Temporal Lobe Epilepsy." British Journal of Psychiatry 117 (1970)

Dewhurst K, Beard AW. Sudden religious conversions in temporal lobe epilepsy. 1970 Epilepsy Behav 2003

Devinsky O, Lai G. Spirituality and religion in epilepsy. Epilepsy Behav 2008.

Devinsky, O., Morrell, MJ, Vogt, BA. (1995) 'Contribution of anterior cingulate cortex to behavior', Brain, 118.

E. Horvitz, "One Hundred Year Study on Artificial Intelligence: Reflections and Framing," ed: Stanford University, 2014.

Eckhart Meister, Selected Writings

Egidi R., ed. (1999), "Von Wright and 'Dante's Dream': Stages in a Philosophical Pilgrim's Progress", in

In Search of a New Humanism: the Philosophy of G.H. von Wright, ed. by R. Egidi, Kluwer, Dordrecht.

Fadiga L, Fogassi L, Pavesi G, Rizzolatti G (1995) Motor facilitation during action observation: a magnetic stimulation study. J Neurophysiol 73: 2608–2611.

Fogassi L, Gallese V, Fadiga L, Rizzolatti G (1998) Neurons responding to the sight of goal directed hand/arm actions in the parietal area PF (7b) of the macaque monkey. Soc Neurosci Abs 24:257.5.

Frith U, Frith CD (2003) Development and neurophysiology of mentalizing. Philos Trans R Soc Lond B Biol Sci 358: 459.

Farah, M.J. (1989), 'The neural basis of mental imagery', Trends in Neurosciences, 10.

Finlay BL, Darlington RB (1995) Linked regularities in the development and evolution of mammalian brains. Science 268.

Freud, S. "The Interpretation of Dreams", 1900

Freud, S. "Selected papers on hysteria and other psychoneuroses" Journal of Nervous and Mental Disease 1909.

Freud, S. "The Origin and Development of Psychoanalysis", 1910

Freud, S. "Psychopathology of everyday life", 1914

Freud, S. "Beyond the Pleasure Principle", 1920

Frith, C.D. & Dolan, R.J. (1997), 'Abnormal beliefs: Delusions and memory', Paper presented at the May, 1997, Harvard Conference on Memory and Belief.

Gay, Volney, ed. Neuroscience and Religion. Plymouth, UK: Lexington Books, 2009.

Gazzaniga, M. S. (1985). The social brain. New York: Basic Books.

Gazzaniga, M.S. (1993), 'Brain mechanisms and conscious experience', Ciba Foundation Symposium, 174.

Geschwind N. "Behavioural changes in temporal lobe epilepsy". Psychol Med. 1979.

Gellhorn, E., Kiely, W.F. "Mystical states of consciousness: neurophysiological and clinical aspects." J Nerv Ment Dis. 1972;154:399-405.

Gilbert SL, Dobyns WB, Lahn BT (2005) Genetic links between brain development and brain evolution. Nat Rev Genet 6.

Gray JA. The Psychology of Fear and Stress. 2nd ed. New York, NY: Cambridge University Press; 1988.

Gloor, P. (1992), 'Amygdala and temporal lobe epilepsy', in The Amygdala: Neurobiological Aspects of Emotion, Memory and Mental Dysfunction, ed J.P. Aggleton (New York: Wiley-Liss).

Greenspan, S. I. and S. G. Shanker (2004). The first idea: How symbols, language, and intelligence evolved from our early primate ancestors to modern humans. Cambridge, MA: Da Capo Press.

Grady, D. (1993), 'The vision thing: Mainly in the brain', Discover, June.

Gallagher HL, Frith CD (2003) Functional imaging of 'theory of mind'. Trends Cogn Sci 7: 77.

Gallese V, Fogassi L, Fadiga L, Rizzolatti G (2002) Action representation and the inferior parietal lobule. In: Prinz W, Hommel B (eds) Attention & Performance XIX. Common mechanisms in perception and action. Oxford University Press, Oxford.

Gallese V, Keysers C, Rizzolatti G (2004) A unifying view of the basis of social cognition. Trends Cogn Sci 8: 396–403.

Goldman AI, Sripada CS (2004) Simulationist models of face-based emotion recognition. Cognition 94: 193–213.

Grèzes J, Costes N, Decety J (1998) Top-down effect of strategy on the perception of human biological motion: a PET investigation. Cogn Neuropsychol 15: 553–582.

Grèzes J, Armony JL, Rowe J, Passingham RE (2003) Activations related to "mirror" and "canonical" neurones in the human brain: an fMRI study. Neuroimage 18: 928–937.

Gross CG, Rocha-Miranda CE, Bender DB (1972) Visual properties of neurons in the inferotemporal cortex of the macaque. J Neurophysiol 35: 96–111.

Guevara Che, The Motorcycle Diaries, 1992

Hari R, Forss N, Avikainen S, Kirveskari S, Salenius S, Rizzolatti G (1998) Activation of human primary motor cortex during action observation: a neuromagnetic study. Proc. Natl Acad Sci USA 95: 15061–15065.

Hardy, G. H. (1940). Ramanujan. Cambridge: Cambridge University Press.

Hall, Daniel, Keith Meador, and Harold Koenig. "Measuring Religiousness in Health Research: Review and Critique." Journal of Religion and Health 47, no. 2 (2008)

Harris, Sam, Jonas Kaplan, Ashley Curiel, Susan Bookheimer, Marco Iacoboni, and Mark Cohen. "The Neural Correlates of Religious and

Nonreligious Belief." PLoS One 4, no. 10 (October 1, 2009)

Halgren, E. (1992), 'Emotional neurophysiology of the amygdala within the context of human cognition', in The Amygdala: Neurobiological Aspects of Emotion, Memory and Mental Dysfunction, ed J.P. Aggleton (New York: Wiley-Liss).

Halligan PW, Fink GR, Marshal JC, Vallar G. 2003. Spatial cognition: evidence from visual neglect. Trends Cogn Sci.

Handbook of Emotions, Edited by Michael Lewis, Jeannette M. Haviland-Jones, and Lisa Feldman Barrett, The Guilford Press; 3rd edition (2010).

Hameroff, S.R. and Penrose, R. (1996) Conscious events as orchestrated space-time selections. Journal of Consciousness Studies 3(1), 36-53; also reprinted in J. Shear (ed.) (1997) Explaining Consciousness-The Hard

Problem. Cambridge, MA, MIT Press, 177-95.

Harding, D.E. (1961) On Having no Head: Zen and the Re-Discovery of the Obvious. London, Buddhist Society.

Hardy, A. (1979) The Spiritual Nature of Man: A Study of Contemporary Religious Experience. Oxford, Clarendon Press.

Harre, R. and Gillett, G. (1994) The Discursive Mind. Thousand Oaks, CA, Sage.

Haugeland, J. (ed.) (1997) Mind Design II: Philosophy, Psychology, Artificial Intelligence. Cambridge, MA, MIT Press.

Hauser, M.D. (2000) Wild Minds: What Animals Really Think. New York, Henry Holt and Co.; London, Penguin.

Hebb, D.O. (1949) The Organization of Behavior. New York, Wiley.

Helmholtz, H.L.F. von (1856-67) Treatise on Physiological Optics.

Hess, EH (1975) "The role of pupil size in communication," Scientific American, 233(5), 110–12.

Heyes, C.M. (1998) Theory of mind in nonhuman primates. Behavioral and Brain Sciences 21, 101-48; with commentaries.

Heyes, C.M. and Galef, B.G. (eds) (1996) Social Learning in Animals: The Roots of Culture. San Diego, CA, Academic Press.

Hilgard, E.R. (1986) Divided Consciousness: Multiple Controls in Human Thought and Action. New York, Wiley.

Hilton, E.N., Lundberg, T.R. Transgender Women in the Female Category of Sport: Perspectives on Testosterone Suppression and Performance Advantage. Sports Med 51, 199–214 (2021).

Hitler, Adolf. Mein Kampf, 1925

Hodgson, R. (1891) A case of double consciousness. Proceedings of the Society for Psychical Research 7, 221-58.

Hofstadter, D.R. and Dennett, D.C. (eds) (1981) The Mind's I: Fantasies and Reflections on Self and Soul. London, Penguin.

Holland, J. (ed.) (2001) Ecstasy: The Complete Guide: A Comprehensive Look at the Risks and Benefits of MDMA. Rochester, VT, Park Street Press.

Holmes, D.S. (1987) The influence of meditation versus rest on physiological arousal. In M. West (ed.) The Psychology of Meditation. Oxford, Clarendon Press, 81-103.

Holmstrom, David. 1992, Christian Science Monitor

Holt, J. (1999) Blindsight in debates about qualia. Journal of Consciousness Studies 6(5), 54-71.

Holloway RL (1996) Evolution of the human brain. In: Lock A, Peters CR (eds) Handbook of human symbolic evolution. Oxford University Press, Oxford

Iacoboni M, Woods RP, Brass M, Bekkering H, Mazziotta JC, Rizzolatti G (1999) Cortical mechanisms of human imitation. Science 286: 2526–2528.

Iacoboni M, Koski LM, Brass M, Bekkering H, Woods RP, Dubeau MC, Mazziotta JC, Rizzolatti G (2001) Reafferent copies of imitated actions in the right superior temporal cortex. Proc Natl Acad Sci USA 98: 13995–13999.

Jeannerod M (1988) The neural and behavioural organization of goal-directed movements. Clarendon Press, Oxford.

Johnson-Frey SH, Maloof FR, Newman-Norlund R, Farrer C, Inati S, Grafton ST (2003) Actions or hand-objects interactions? Human inferior frontal cortex and action observation. Neuron 39: 1053–1058.

Jackson, F. (1982) Epiphenomenal qualia. Philosophical Quarterly 32, 127-36.

James, W. (1890) The Principles of Psychology (2 volumes). London, Macmillan.

James, W. (1902) The Varieties of Religious Experience: A Study in Human Nature. New York and London, Longmans, Green and Co.

Jansen, K. (2001) Ketamine: Dreams and Realities. Sarasota, FL, Multidisciplinary Association for Psychedelic Studies.

Jay, M. (ed.) (1999) Artificial Paradises: A Drugs Reader. London, Penguin.

Jaynes, J. (1976) The Origin of Consciousness in the Breakdown of the Bicameral Mind. New York, Houghton Mifflin.

Johnson, M.K. and Raye, C.L. (1981) Reality monitoring. Psychological Review 88, 67-85.

Kadim I, Mahgoub O, Baqir S et al. (2015) Cultured meat from muscle stem cells: a review of challenges and prospects. J Integr Agr 14: 222–233

Kandel, E. R. In Search of Memory: The Emergence of a New Science of Mind, W. W. Norton & Company (2007).

Kandel E. R. Schwartz JH, Jessel TM. Principles of neural sciences. New York; McGraw Hill, 2000.

Kanwisher, N. (2001) Neural events and perceptual awareness. Cognition

79, 89-113; also reprinted inS. Dehaene (ed.) The Cognitive Neuroscience of Consciousness. Cambridge, MA, MIT Press, 89-113.

Karn, K. and Hayhoe, M. (2000) Memory representations guide targeting eye movements in a natural task. Visual Cognition 7, 673-703.

Kennedy, H., & Dehay, C. (1988). Functional implications of the anatomical organization of the callosal projections of visual areas V1 and V2 in the macaque monkey. Behav. Brain Res., 29, 225–236.

Kentridge, R.W. and Heywood, C.A. (1999) The status of blindsight. Journal of Consciousness Studies 6(5), 3-11.

Kihlstrom, J.F. (1996) Perception without awareness of what is perceived, learning without awareness of what is learned. In M. Velmans (ed.) The Science of Consciousness. London, Routledge, 23-46.

Kosslyn, S.M. (1980) Image and Mind. Cambridge, MA, Harvard University Press.

Kosslyn, S.M. (1988) Aspects of a cognitive neuroscience of mental imagery. Science 240, 1621-6.

Kinsbourne, M. (1995), 'The intralaminar thalamic nucleii', Consciousness and Cognition, 4.

Kjaer, Troels, Camilla Bertelsen, Paola Piccini, David Brooks, Jorgen Alving, and Hans Lou. "Increased Dopamine Tone during Meditation- Induced Change of Consciousness." Cognitive Brain Research 13, no. 2 (April 2002)

Kölmel HW. 1985. Complex visual hallucinations in the hemianopic field. J Neurol Neurosurg Psychiatry.

Koenig, Harold. "Research on Religion, Spirituality, and Mental Health: A Review." Canadian Journal of Psychiatry 54, no. 5 (May 2009)

Koenig, Harold, ed. Handbook of Religion and Mental Health. San Diego, CA: Academic Press, 1998

Kraepelin E. Psychiatry: A Textbook for Students and Physicians. New York, NY: Science History Publications; 1990.

Lauglin, Charles, John McManus, and Eugene d'Aquili. Brain, Symbol, and Experience. 2nd ed. New York: Columbia University Press, 1992

Lakoff, G. and M. Johnson (1999). Philosophy in the flesh. Basic Books: New York.

LeDoux, J. E. (1996). The emotional brain. New York: Simon & Schuster.

LeDoux, J.E. (1992), 'Emotion and the amygdala', in The Amygdala: Neurobiological Aspects of Emo- tion, Memory and Mental Dysfunction, ed J.P. Aggleton (New York: Wiley-Liss).

Levin, D.T. and Simons, D.J. (1997) Failure to detect changes to attended objects in motion pictures. Psychonomic Bulletin and Review 4, 501-6.

Levine,J. (1983) Materialism and qualia: the explanatory gap. Pacific Philosophical Quarterly 64, 354-61.

Levine,J. (2001) Purple Haze: The Puzzle of Consciousness. New York, Oxford University Press. Levine, S. (1979) A Gradual Awakening. New York, Doubleday.

Levinson, B.W. (1965) States of awareness during general anaesthesia. British Journal of Anaesthesia 37, 544-6.

Lewicki, P., Czyzewska, M. and Hoffman, H. (1987) Unconscious acquisition of complex procedural knowledge. Journal of Experimental Psychology: Learning, Memory and Cognition 13, 523-30.

Lewicki, P., Hill, T. and Bizot, E. (1988) Acquisition of procedural knowledge about a pattern of stimuli that cannot be articulated. Cognitive Psychology 20, 24-37.

Lewicki, P., Hill, T. and Czyzewska, M. (1992) Nonconscious acquisition of information. American Psychologist 47, 796-801.

Manthey S, Schubotz RI, von Cramon DY (2003). Premotor cortex in observing erroneous action: an fMRI study. Brain Res Cogn Brain Res 15: 296–307.

Mesulam MM, Mufson EJ (1982) Insula of the old world monkey. III: Efferent cortical output and comments on function. J Comp Neurol 212: 38–52.

Naskar, Abhijit. "Homo: A Brief History of Consciousness", 2015

Naskar, Abhijit. "What is Mind?", 2016

Naskar, Abhijit. "Love, God & Neurons: Memoir of A Scientist who found himself by getting lost", 2016

Naskar, Abhijit. "Principia Humanitas", 2017

Naskar, Abhijit. "We Are All Black: A Treatise on Racism", 2017

Naskar, Abhijit. "Either Civilized or Phobic: A Treatise on Homosexuality", 2017

Naskar, Abhijit. "The Bengal Tigress: A Treatise on Gender Equality", 2017

Naskar, Abhijit. "Morality Absolute", 2017

Naskar, Abhijit. "Build Bridges not Walls: In the name of Americana", 2018

Naskar, Abhijit. "Fabric of Humanity", 2018

Naskar, Abhijit. "Citizens of Peace: Beyond the Savagery of Sovereignty", 2019

Naskar, Abhijit. "The Constitution of The United Peoples of Earth", 2019

Naskar, Abhijit. "Neurons Giveth, Neurons Taketh Away | Abhijit Naskar | TEDxIIMRanchi", 2019 https://www.youtube.com/watch?v=B NX-Q0ySm80

Naskar, Abhijit. "Mission Reality", 2019

Naskar, Abhijit. "Operation Justice: To Make A Society That Needs No Law", 2019

Naskar, Abhijit. "Every Generation Needs Caretakers: The Gospel of Patriotism", 2020

Naskar, Abhijit. "Hurricane Humans: Give me accountability, I'll give you peace", 2020

Naskar, Abhijit. "Revolution Indomable", 2020

Naskar, Abhijit. "Servitude is Sanctitude", 2020

Naskar, Abhijit. "Good Scientist: When Science and Service Combine", 2020

Newberg, Andrew, and Jeremy Iversen. "The Neural Basis of the Complex Mental Task of Meditation: Neurotransmitter and Neurochemical Considerations." Medical Hypotheses 61, no. 2 (2003).

Newberg, Andrew. "How God Changes Your Brain: An Introduction to Jewish Neurotheology", CCAR Journal: The Reform Jewish Quarterly, Winter 2016.

Newberg, Andrew, and Stephanie Newberg. "A Neuropsychological Perspective on Spiritual Development." In Handbook of Spiritual Development in Childhood and Adolescence, edited by Eugene

Roehlkepartain, Pamela King, Linda Wagener, and Peter Benson. London: Sage Publications, Inc., 2005

Newberg, Andrew. "The Neurotheology Link An Intersection Between Spirituality and Health", Alternative and Complimentary Therapies, Vol 21 No 1, February 2015.

Newberg, Andrew, Nancy Wintering, Dharma Khalsa, Hannah Roggenkamp, and Mark Waldman. "Meditation Effects on Cognitive Function and Cerebral Blood Flow in Subjects with Memory Loss: A Preliminary Study." Journal of Alzheimer's Disease 20, no. 2 (2010)

Nash, M. (1995), 'Glimpses of the mind', Time.

Nesse RM. Proximate and evolutionary studies of anxiety, stress and depression: synergy at the interface. Neurosci Biobehav Rev. 1999;23:895-903.

Nicolelis, Miguel. (2011) "Beyond Boundaries: The New Neuroscience of Connecting Brains with Machines---and How It Will Change Our Lives", Times Books

O'Hara, K. and Scutt, T. (1996) There is no hard problem of consciousness. Journal of Consciousness Studies 3(4), 290-302, reprinted in J. Shear (ed.) (1997) Explaining Consciousness. Cambridge, MA, MIT Press, 69-82.

O'Regan, J.K. (1992) Solving the "real" mysteries of visual perception: the world as an outside memory. Canadian Journal of Psychology 46, 461-88.

O'Regan, J.K. and Noe, A. (2001) A sensorimotor account of vision and visual consciousness. Behavioral and Brain Sciences 24(5), 883-917.

O'Regan, J.K., Rensink, R.A. and Clark,].]. (1999) Change-blindness as a result of "mudsplashes." Nature 398, 34.

Ornstein, R.E. (1977) The Psychology of Consciousness (2nd edn). New York, Harcourt.

Ornstein, R.E. (1986) The Psychology of Consciousness (3rd edn). New York, Pehguin.

Ornstein, R.E. (1992) The Evolution of Consciousness. New York, Touchstone.

Penfield W, Faulk ME (1955) The insula: further observations on its function. Brain 78: 445– 470.

Penrose, R. (1994), Shadows of the Mind (Oxford: Oxford University Press).

Penrose, R. (1989), The Emperor's New Mind: Concerning Computers, Minds and The Laws of Physics (Oxford: Oxford University Press).

Persinger, "'I would kill in God's name' role of sex, weekly church attendance, report of a religious experience and limbic lability" Perceptual and Motor Skills 1997.

Persinger "Experimental simulation of the God experience" Neurotheology 2003.

Persinger, Corradini, Clement, Keaney, et al "Neurotheology and its convergence with neuroquantology" NeuroQuantology 2010.

Persinger, Koren and St-Pierre "The electromagnetic induction of mystical and altered states within the laboratory" Journal of Consciousness Exploration and Research 2010.

Persinger "Case report: A prototypical spontaneous 'sensed presence' of a sentient being and concomitant electroencephalographic activity in the clinical laboratory" Neurocase 2008.

Persinger and Saroka "Potential production of Hughlings Jackson's "parasitic consciousness" by physiologically-patterned weak transcerebral magnetic fields: QEEG and source localization" Epilepsy & Behavior 28 (2013).

Persinger. "The neuropsychiatry of paranormal experiences". J Neuropsychiatry Clin Neurosci 2001.

Persinger. "Neuropsychological bases of god beliefs", New York: Praeger, 1987

Persinger. "Temporal lobe epileptic signs and correlative behaviors displayed by normal populations", Journal of General Psychology, 1986

Perry BD, Pollard R. Homeostasis, stress, trauma, and adaptation. A neurodevelopmental view of childhood trauma. Child Adolesc Psychiatr Clin N Am. 1998;7:33.

Paré, D. & Llinás, R. (1995), 'Conscious and preconscious processes as seen from the standpoint of sleep-waking cycle neurophysiology', Neuropsychologia, 33.

Phillips ML, Young AW, Senior C, Brammer M, Andrew C, Calder AJ, Bullmore ET, Perrett DI, Rowland D, Williams SC, Gray JA, David AS (1997) A specific neural substrate for perceiving facial expressions of disgust. Nature 389: 495–498.

Phillips ML, Young AW, Scott SK, Calder AJ, Andrew C, Giampietro V, Williams SC, Bullmore ET, Brammer M, Gray JA (1998) Neural responses to facial and vocal expressions of fear and disgust. Proc R Soc Lond B Biol Sci 265: 1809–1817.

Puce A, Perrett D (2003) Electrophysiological and brain imaging of biological motion. Philosoph Trans Royal Soc Lond, Series B, 358: 435–445.

Ramachandran VS. Behavioral and magnetoencephalographic correlates of plasticity in the adult human brain. Proc Natl Acad Sci USA 1993; 90: 10413–20.

Ramachandran VS. Phantom limbs, neglect syndromes, repressed memories, and Freudian psychology. Int Rev Neurobiol 1994; 37: 291–333.

Ramachandran VS. Plasticity and functional recovery in neurology. Clin Med 2005; 5: 368–73.

Ramachandran VS, Hirstein W. The perception of phantom limbs. The D. O. Hebb lecture. Brain 1998; 121: 1603–30.

Ramachandran VS, Rogers-Ramachandran D, Cobb S. Touching the phantom limb. Nature 1995; 377: 489–90.

Ramachandran VS, Rogers-Ramachandran D. Phantom limbs and

neural plasticity. Arch Neurol 2000; 57: 317–20.

Ramachandran VS, Rogers-Ramachandran D. It's all done with mirrors. Sci Am Mind 2007; 18: 16–9.

Ramachandran VS, Rogers-Ramachandran D. Sensations referred to a patient's phantom arm from another subjects intact arm: perceptual correlates of mirror neurons. Med Hypotheses 2008; 70: 1233–4.

Ramachandran VS, Rogers-Ramachandran D, Stewart M. Perceptual correlates of massive cortical reorganization. Science 1992; 258: 1159–60.

Rizzolatti G, Craighero L (2004) The mirror-neuron system. Annu Rev Neurosci 27: 169–192.

Rizzolatti G, Fogassi L, Gallese V (2001) Neurophysiological mechanisms underlying the understanding and imitation of action. Nature Rev Neurosci 2:661–670.

Rock I, Victor J. Vision and touch: an experimentally created conflict between the two senses. Science 1964; 143: 594–6.

Rose´n B, Lundborg G. Training with a mirror in rehabilitation of the hand. Scand J Plast Reconstr Surg Hand Surg 2005; 39: 104–8.

Roberts, TA; Smalley, J; Ahrendt, D (December 2020). "Effect of gender affirming hormones on athletic performance in transwomen and transmen: implications for sporting organisations and legislators". British Journal of Sports Medicine. 55 (11): 577–583

Royet JP, Plailly J, Delon-Martin C, Kareken DA, Segebarth C (2003) fMRI of emotional responses to odors: influence of hedonic valence and judgment, handedness, and gender. Neuroimage 20: 713–728.

Rozin R Haidt J and McCauley CR (2000) Disgust. In: Lewis M, Haviland-Jones JM (eds) Handbook of Emotion. 2nd Edition. Guilford Press, New York, pp 637–653.

Saxe R, Carey S, Kanwisher N (2004) Understanding other minds: linking developmental psychology and functional neuroimaging. Annu Rev Psychol 55: 87–124.

S. J. Russell and P. Norvig, Artificial intelligence: a modern approach (3rd edition): Prentice Hall, 2009.

Singer T, Seymour B, O'Doherty J, Kaube H, Dolan RJ, Frith CD (2004) Empathy for pain involves the affective but not the sensory components of pain. Science 303: 1157–1162.

Smith A (1759) The theory of moral sentiments (ed. 1976). Clarendon Press, Oxford.

Schilling, Vincent. 2017, indian country today

Stein, Stephen K. 2017, The Sea in World History: Exploration, Travel, and Trade

Simonsen R (2015) Eating for the future: veganism and the challenge of in vitro meat. In: Stapleton P, Byers A (Hg). Biopolitics and utopia. Palgrave Macmillan, New York (2015), S 167–190

Tesla N. "My Inventions", 1919

T. R. Society, "Machine learning: the power and promise of computers that learn by example," ed. The Royal Society, 2017.

Tomasello M, Call J (1997) Primate cognition. Oxford University Press, Oxford.

www.ingramcontent.com/pod-product-compliance
Lightning Source LLC
Chambersburg PA
CBHW051047250726
48656CB00001B/182